DUINO
ELEGIES

RAINER MARIA RILKE

DUINO
ELEGIES

Translated by
STEPHEN MITCHELL

Unabridged

SHAMBHALA
Boston
1992

Shambhala Publications, Inc.
Horticultural Hall
300 Massachusetts Avenue
Boston, Massachusetts 02115

9 8 7 6 5 4 3 2 1

First Shambhala Edition
Printed in Hong Kong on acid-free paper ⊚
Distributed in the United States by Random House, Inc.,
in Canada by Random House of Canada Ltd.

Cover art: *Family of Saltimbanques* by Pablo Picasso.
Chester Dale Collection, © National Gallery
of Art, Washington, D.C.

See page 116 for Library of Congress
Cataloging-in-Publication data.

CONTENTS

DUINO ELEGIES

*The property of
Princess Marie von Thurn
und Taxis-Hohenlohe*

THE FIRST ELEGY

Who, if I cried out, would hear me
    among the angels'
hierarchies? and even if one of them
    pressed me
suddenly against his heart: I would be
    consumed
in that overwhelming existence. For
    beauty is nothing
but the beginning of terror, which we
    still are just able to endure,
and we are so awed because it serenely
    disdains
to annihilate us. Every angel is
    terrifying.
    And so I hold myself back and
    swallow the call-note

of my dark sobbing. Ah, whom can we
      ever turn to
in our need? Not angels, not humans,
and already the knowing animals are
      aware
that we are not really at home in
our interpreted world. Perhaps there
      remains for us
some tree on a hillside, which every
      day we can take
into our vision; there remains for us
      yesterday's street
and the loyalty of a habit so much
      at ease
when it stayed with us that it moved
      in and never left.
   Oh and night: there is night, when
      a wind full of infinite space
gnaws at our faces. Whom would it
      not remain for—that longed-
      after,

mildly disillusioning presence, which
    the solitary heart
so painfully meets. Is it any less
    difficult for lovers?
But they keep on using each other
    to hide their own fate.
    Don't you know *yet*? Fling the
    emptiness out of your arms
into the spaces we breathe; perhaps
    the birds
will feel the expanded air with more
    passionate flying.

Yes—the springtimes needed you.
    Often a star
was waiting for you to notice it.
    A wave rolled toward you
out of the distant past, or as you
    walked
under an open window, a violin
yielded itself to your hearing. All this
    was mission.

But could you accomplish it? Weren't
    you always
distracted by expectation, as if every
    event
announced a beloved? (Where can you
    find a place
to keep her, with all the huge strange
    thoughts inside you
going and coming and often staying
    all night.)
But when you feel longing, sing of
    women in love;
for their famous passion is still not
    immortal. Sing
of women abandoned and desolate
    (you envy them, almost)
who could love so much more purely
    than those who were gratified.
Begin again and again the never-
    attainable praising;
remember: the hero lives on; even his
    downfall was

merely a pretext for achieving his
    final birth.
But Nature, spent and exhausted,
    takes lovers back
into herself, as if there were not
    enough strength
to create them a second time. I have
    you imagined
Gaspara Stampa intensely enough so
    that any girl
deserted by her beloved might be
    inspired
by that fierce example of soaring,
    objectless love
and might say to herself, "Perhaps I
    can be like her?"
Shouldn't this most ancient of suf-
    ferings finally grow
more fruitful for us? Isn't it time that
    we lovingly
freed ourselves from the beloved and,
    quivering, endured:

as the arrow endures the bowstring's
    tension, so that
gathered in the snap of release it can
    be more than
itself. For there is no place where we
    can remain.

Voices. Voices. Listen, my heart, as
    only
saints have listened: until the gigantic
    call lifted them
off the ground; yet they kept on,
    impossibly,
kneeling and didn't notice at all:
so complete was their listening. Not
    that you could endure
God's voice—far from it. But listen to
    the voice of the wind
and the ceaseless message that forms
    itself out of silence.
It is murmuring toward you now from
    those who died young.

Didn't their fate, whenever you
    stepped into a church
in Naples or Rome, quietly come to
    address you?
Or high up, some eulogy entrusted
    you with a mission,
as, last year, on the plaque in Santa
    Maria Formosa.
What they want of me is that I gently
    remove the appearance
of injustice about their death—which
    at times
slightly hinders their souls from pro
    ceeding onward.

Of course, it is strange to inhabit the
    earth no longer,
to give up customs one barely had
    time to learn,
not to see roses and other promising
    Things

in terms of a human future; no longer
    to be
what one was in infinitely anxious
    hands; to leave
even one's own first name behind,
    forgetting it
as easily as a child abandons a broken
    toy.
Strange to no longer desire one's
    desires. Strange
to see meanings that clung together
    once, floating away
in every direction. And being dead is
    hard work
and full of retrieval before one can
    gradually feel
a trace of eternity.—Though the living
    are wrong to believe
in the too-sharp distinctions which
    they themselves have created.
Angels (they say) don't know whether
    it is the living

they are moving among, or the dead.
        The eternal torrent
whirls all ages along in it, through
        both realms
forever, and their voices are drowned
        out in its thunderous roar.

In the end, those who were carried off
        early no longer need us:
they are weaned from earth's sorrows
        and joys, as gently as children
outgrow the soft breasts of their
        mothers. But we, who do need
such great mysteries, we for whom
        grief is so often
the source of our spirit's growth —:
        could we exist without *them*?
Is the legend meaningless that tells
        how, in the lament for Linus,
the daring first notes of song pierced
        through the barren numbness;

and then in the startled space which a
    youth as lovely as a god
had suddenly left forever, the Void felt
    for the first time
that harmony which now enraptures
    and comforts and helps us.

THE SECOND ELEGY

Every angel is terrifying. And yet, alas,
I invoke you, almost deadly birds of
        the soul,
knowing about you. Where are the
        days of Tobias,
when one of you, veiling his radiance,
        stood at the front door,
slightly disguised for the journey, no
        longer appalling;
(a young man like the one who cur-
        iously peeked through the
        window).
But if the archangel now, perilous,
        from behind the stars
took even one step down toward us:
        our own heart, beating

higher and higher, would beat us to
      death. Who *are* you?

Early successes, Creation's pampered
      favorites,
mountain-ranges, peaks growing red in
      the dawn
of all Beginning,—pollen of the flow-
      ering godhead,
joints of pure light, corridors, stair-
      ways, thrones,
space formed from essence, shields
      made of ecstasy, storms
of emotion whirled into rapture, and
      suddenly, alone:
mirrors, which scoop up the beauty that
      has streamed from their face
and gather it back, into themselves,
      entire.

But we, when moved by deep feeling,
      evaporate; we

breathe ourselves out and away; from
    moment to moment
our emotion grows fainter, like a
    perfume. Though someone may
    tell us:
"Yes, you've entered my bloodstream,
    the room, the whole springtime
is filled with you . . ."—what does it
    matter? he can't contain us,
we vanish inside him and around him
    And those who are beautiful,
oh who can retain them? Appearance
    ceaselessly rises
in their face, and is gone. Like dew
    from the morning grass,
what is ours floats into the air, like
    steam from a dish
of hot food. O smile, where are you
    going? O upturned glance:
new warm receding wave on the sea
    of the heart . . .

alas, but that is what we *are.* Does the
    infinite space
we dissolve into, taste of us then? Do
    the angels really
reabsorb only the radiance that
    streamed out from themselves, or
sometimes, as if by an oversight, is
    there a trace
of our essence in it as well? Are we
    mixed in with their
features even as slightly as that vague
    look
in the faces of pregnant women? They
    do not notice it
(how could they notice) in their
    swirling return to themselves.

Lovers, if they knew how, might utter
    strange, marvelous
words in the night air. For it seems
    that everything

hides us. Look: trees do exist; the
    houses
that we live in still stand. We alone
fly past all things, as fugitive as the
    wind.
And all things conspire to keep silent
    about us, half
out of shame perhaps, half as unut-
    terable hope.

Lovers, gratified in each other, I am
    asking *you*
about us. You hold each other. Where
    is your proof?
Look, sometimes I find that my hands
    have become aware
of each other, or that my time-worn
    face
shelters itself inside them. That gives
    me a slight
sensation. But who would dare to
    exist, just for that?

You, though, who in the other's
    passion
grow until, overwhelmed, he begs you:
"No *more* . . ."; you who beneath his
    hands
swell with abundance, like autumn
    grapes;
you who may disappear because the
    other has wholly
emerged: I am asking *you* about us.
    I know,
you touch so blissfully because the
    caress preserves,
because the place you so tenderly
    cover
does not vanish; because underneath it
you feel pure duration. So you promise
    eternity, almost,
from the embrace. And yet, when you
    have survived
the terror of the first glances, the
    longing at the window,

and the first walk together, once only,
    through the garden:
lovers, *are* you the same? When you
    lift yourselves up
to each other's mouth and your lips
    join, drink against drink:
oh how strangely each drinker seeps
    away from his action.

Weren't you astonished by the caution
    of human gestures   .
on Attic gravestones? Wasn't love and
    departure
placed so gently on shoulders that it
    seemed to be made
of a different substance than in our
    world? Remember the hands,
how weightlessly they rest, though
    there is power in the torsos.
These self-mastered figures know:
    "We can go this far,

this is ours, to touch one another this
        lightly; the gods
can press down harder upon us. But
        that is the gods' affair."

If only we too could discover a pure,
        contained,
human place, our own strip of fruit-
        bearing soil
between river and rock. For our own
        heart always exceeds us,
as theirs did. And we can no longer
        follow it, gazing
into images that soothe it or into the
        godlike bodies
where, measured more greatly, it
        achieves a greater repose.

THE THIRD ELEGY

It is one thing to sing the beloved.
    Another, alas,
to invoke that hidden, guilty river-god
    of the blood.
Her young lover, whom she knows
    from far away—what does he
    know of
the lord of desire who often, up from
    the depths of his solitude,
even before she could soothe him, and
    as though she didn't exist,
held up his head, ah, dripping with the
    unknown,
erect, and summoned the night to an
    endless uproar.
Oh the Neptune inside our blood, with
    his appalling trident.

Oh the dark wind from his breast out
      of that spiraled conch.
Listen to the night as it makes itself
      hollow. O stars,
isn't it from you that the lover's desire
      for the face
of his beloved arises? Doesn't his secret
      insight
into her pure features come from the
      pure constellations?

Not you, his mother: alas, you were
      not the one
who bent the arch of his eyebrows
      into such expectation.
Not for you, girl so aware of him, not
      for your mouth
did his lips curve themselves into a
      more fruitful expression.
Do you really think that your gentle
      steps could have shaken him

with such violence, you who move like
    the morning breeze?
Yes, you did frighten his heart; but
    more ancient terrors
plunged into him at the shock of that
    feeling. Call him . . .
but you can't quite call him away from
    those dark companions.
Of course, he *wants* to escape, and he
    does; relieved, he nestles
into your sheltering heart, takes hold,
    and begins himself.
But did he ever begin himself, really?
Mother, *you* made him small, it was
    you who started him;
in *your* sight he was new, over his new
    eyes you arched
the friendly world and warded off the
    world that was alien.
Ah, where are the years when you
    shielded him just by placing

your slender form between him and
    the surging abyss?
How much you hid from him then.
    The room that filled with sus-
    picion
at night: you made it harmless; and
    out of the refuge of your heart
you mixed a more human space in
    with his night-space.
And you set down the lamp, not in
    that darkness, but in
your own nearer presence, and it
    glowed at him like a friend.
There wasn't a creak that your smile
    could not explain,
as though you had long known just
    when the floor would do that . . .
And he listened and was soothed.
    So powerful was your presence
as you tenderly stood by the bed; his
    fate,

tall and cloaked, retreated behind the
     wardrobe, and his restless
future, delayed for a while, adapted to
     the folds of the curtain.

And he himself, as he lay there, re-
     lieved, with the sweetness
of the gentle world you had made for
     him dissolving beneath
his drowsy eyelids, into the foretaste
     of sleep—:
he *seemed* protected . . . But inside:
     who could ward off,
who could divert, the floods of origin
     inside him?
Ah, there *was* no trace of caution in
     that sleeper; sleeping,
yes but dreaming, but flushed with
     what fevers; how he threw him-
     self in.
All at once new, trembling, how he
     was caught up

and entangled in the spreading tendrils
    of inner event
already twined into patterns, into
    strangling undergrowth, prowling
bestial shapes. How he submitted—.
    Loved.
Loved his interior world, his interior
    wilderness,
that primal forest inside him, where
    among decayed treetrunks
his heart stood, light-green. Loved.
    Left it, went through
his own roots and out, into the pow-
    erful source
where his little birth had already been
    outlived. Loving,
he waded down into more ancient
    blood, to ravines
where Horror lay, still glutted with his
    fathers. And every
Terror knew him, winked at him like
    an accomplice.

Yes, Atrocity smiled . . . Seldom
had you smiled so tenderly, mother.
    How could he help
loving what smiled at him. Even before
    he knew you,
he had loved it, for already while you
    carried him inside you, it
was dissolved in the water that makes
    the embryo weightless.

No, we don't accomplish our love in a
    single year
as the flowers do; an immemorial sap
flows up through our arms when we
    love. Dear girl,
this: that we loved, inside us, not One
    who would someday appear, but
seething multitudes; not just a single
    child,
but also the fathers lying in our depths
like fallen mountains; also the dried-up
    riverbeds

of ancient mothers—; also the whole
soundless landscape under the clouded
    or clear
sky of its destiny—; all this, my dear,
    preceded you.

And you yourself, how could you
    know
what primordial time you stirred in
    your lover. What passions
welled up inside him from departed
    beings. What
women hated you there. How many
    dark
sinister men you aroused in his young
    veins. Dead
children reached out to touch you . . .
    Oh gently, gently,
let him see you performing, with love,
    some confident daily task,—

lead him out close to the garden, give
    him what outweighs
the heaviest night . . . . . .
                Restrain him . . . . . .

THE FOURTH ELEGY

O trees of life, when does your winter
    come?
We are not in harmony, our blood
    does not forewarn us
like migratory birds'. Late, overtaken,
we force ourselves abruptly onto the
    wind
and fall to earth at some iced-over
    lake.
Flowering and fading come to us both
    at once.
And somewhere lions still roam and
    never know,
in their majestic power, of any weak-
    ness.

But we, while we are intent upon one
    object,

already feel the pull of another. Con-
flict
is second nature to us. Aren't lovers
always arriving at each other's
        boundaries?—
although they promised vastness,
        hunting, home.
    As when for some quick sketch,
        a wide background
of contrast is laboriously prepared
so that we can see more clearly:
        we never know
the actual, vital contour of our own
emotions—just what forms them
        from outside.
    Who has not sat, afraid, before
        his heart's
curtain? It rose: the scenery of
        farewell.
Easy to recognize. The well-known
        garden,

which swayed a little. Then the dancer
came.
Not *him*. Enough! However lightly he
moves,
he's costumed, made up— an ordinary
man
who hurries home and walks in
through the kitchen.
  I won't endure these half-filled
human masks;
better, the puppet. It at least is full.
I'll put up with the stuffed skin, the
wire, the face
that is nothing but appearance. Here.
I'm waiting.
Even if the lights go out; even if someone
tells me "That's all"; even if emptiness
floats toward me in a gray draft from
the stage;
even if not one of my silent ancestors

stays seated with me, not one woman,
     not
the boy with the immovable brown
     eye—
I'll sit here anyway. One can always
     watch.

Am I not right? You, to whom life
     tasted
so bitter after you took a sip of mine,
the first, gritty infusion of my will,
Father—who, as I grew up, kept on
     tasting
and, troubled by the aftertaste of so
strange a future, searched my unfo-
     cused gaze—
you who, so often since you died,
     have trembled
for my well-being, within my deepest
     hope,
relinquishing that calmness which the
     dead

feel as their very essence, countless
    realms
of equanimity, for my scrap of life—
tell me, am I not right? And you,
    dear women
who must have loved me for my small
    beginning
of love toward you, which I always
    turned away from
because the space in your features
    grew, changed,
even while I loved it, into cosmic
    space,
where you no longer were—: am I
    not right
to feel as if I *must* stay seated, must
wait before the puppet stage, or,
    rather,
gaze at it so intensely that at last,
to balance my gaze, an angel has to
    come and
make the stuffed skins startle into life.

Angel and puppet: a real play, finally.
Then what we separate by our very
          presence
can come together. And only then,
          the whole
cycle of transformation will arise,
out of our own life-seasons. Above,
          beyond us,
the angel plays. If no one else, the
          dying
must notice how unreal, how full
          of pretense,
is all that we accomplish here,
          where nothing
is allowed to be itself. Oh hours of
          childhood,
when behind each shape more than
          the past appeared
and what streamed out before us
          was not the future.
We felt our bodies growing and were
          at times

impatient to *be* grown up, half for
    the sake
of those with nothing left but their
    grownupness.
Yet were, when playing by ourselves,
    enchanted
with what alone endures; and we
    would stand there
in the infinite, blissful space between
    world and toy,
at a point which, from the earliest
    beginning,
had been established for a pure event.

Who shows a child as he really is?
    Who sets him
in his constellation and puts the
    measuring-rod
of distance in his hand? Who makes
    his death
out of gray bread, which hardens—
    or leaves it there

inside his round mouth, jagged as
    the core
of a sweet apple? . . . . . . Murderers
    are easy
to understand. But this: that one can
    contain
death, the whole of death, even before
life has begun, can hold it to one's
    heart
gently, and not refuse to go on living,
is inexpressible.

THE FIFTH ELEGY

Dedicated to Frau Hertha Koenig

But tell me, who *are* they, these wan-
    derers, even more
transient than we ourselves, who from
    their earliest days
are savagely wrung out
by a never-satisfied will (for *whose*
    sake)? Yet it wrings them,
bends them, twists them, swings them
    and flings them
and catches them again; and falling as
    if through oiled
slippery air, they land
on the threadbare carpet, worn con-
    stantly thinner
by their perpetual leaping, this carpet
    that is lost

in infinite space.
Stuck on like a bandage, as if the sub-
     urban sky
had wounded the earth.
          And hardly has it appeared
when, standing there, upright, is: the
     large capital D
that begins Duration . . . , and the
     always-approaching grip
takes them again, as a joke, even the
     strongest
men, and crushes them, the way King
     Augustus the Strong
would crush a pewter plate.

Ah and around this
center: the rose of Onlooking
blooms and unblossoms. Around this
pestle pounding the carpet,
this pistil, fertilized by the pollen
of its own dust, and producing in turn

the specious fruit of displeasure:
        the unconscious
gaping faces, their thin
surfaces glossy with boredom's
        specious half-smile.

There: the shriveled-up, wrinkled
        weight-lifter,
an old man who only drums now,
shrunk in his enormous skin, which
        looks as if it had once
contained *two* men, and the other
were already lying in the graveyard,
        while this one lived on with-
        out him,
deaf and sometimes a little
confused, in the widowed skin.

And the young one over there, the
        man, who might be the son of
        a neck
and a nun: firm and vigorously filled

with muscles and innocence.

Children,
whom a grief that was still quite small
once received as a toy, during one
　　　of its
long convalescences . . . .

You, little boy, who fall down
a hundred times daily, with the thud
that only unripe fruits know, from
　　　the tree of mutually
constructed motion (which more
　　　quickly than water, in a few
minutes, has its spring, summer, and
　　　autumn)—
fall down hard on the grave:
sometimes, during brief pauses,
　　　a loving look
toward your seldom affectionate
　　　mother tries to be born

in your expression; but it gets lost
    along the way,
your body consumes it, that timid
scarcely-attempted face . . . And again
the man is clapping his hands for your
    leap, and before
a pain can become more distinct near
    your constantly racing
heart, the stinging in your soles rushes
    ahead of
that other pain, chasing a pair
of physical tears quickly into your
    eyes.
And nevertheless, blindly,
the smile . . . . .

Oh gather it, Angel, that small-
    flowered herb of healing.
Create a vase and preserve it. Set it
    among those joys
not *yet* open to us; on that lovely urn

praise it with the ornately flowing
    inscription:
             "Subrisio Saltat."
  And you then, my lovely darling,
you whom the most tempting joys
have mutely leapt over. Perhaps
your fringes are happy *for* you—,
or perhaps the green
metallic silk stretched over your firm
    young breasts
feels itself endlessly indulged and in
    need of nothing.
You
display-fruit of equanimity,
set out in front of the public, in con-
    tinual variations
on all the swaying scales of equipoise,
lifted among the shoulders.

Oh *where* is the place—I carry it in
    my heart—,

where they still were far from mastery,
    still fell apart
from each other, like mating cattle
    that someone
has badly paired;—
where the weights are still heavy;
    where
from their vainly twirling sticks
the plates still wobble
and drop . . . . .

And suddenly in this laborious no-
    where, suddenly
the unsayable spot where the pure
    Too-little is transformed
incomprehensibly—, leaps around
    and changes
into that empty Too-much;
where the difficult calculation
becomes numberless and resolved.

Squares, oh square in Paris, infinite
    showplace
where the milliner Madame Lamort
twists and winds the restless paths of
    the earth,
those endless ribbons, and, from them,
    designs
new bows, frills, flowers, ruffles, arti-
    ficial fruits—, all
falsely colored,—for the cheap
winter bonnets of Fate.

. . . .

Angel!: If there were a place that we
    didn't know of, and there,
on some unsayable carpet, lovers dis-
    played
what they never could bring to mas-
    tery here—the bold
exploits of their high-flying hearts,
their towers of pleasure, their ladders

that have long since been standing
    where there was no ground,
    leaning
just on each other, trembling,—and
    could *master* all this,
before the surrounding spectators, the
    innumerable soundless dead:
  Would these, then, throw down
    their final, forever saved-up,
forever hidden, unknown to us,
    eternally valid
coins of happiness before the at last
genuinely smiling pair on the gratified
carpet?

THE SIXTH ELEGY

Fig-tree, for such a long time I have
    ·   found meaning
in the way you almost completely omit
    your blossoms
and urge your pure mystery, unpro-
    claimed,
into the early ripening fruit.
Like the curved pipe of a fountain,
    your arching boughs drive the
    sap
downward and up again: and almost
    without awakening
it bursts out of sleep, into its sweetest
    achievement.
Like the god stepping into the swan.
    . . . . . . But *we* still linger, alas,

we, whose pride is in blossoming; we
      enter the overdue
interior of our final fruit and are al-
      ready betrayed.
In only a few does the urge to action
      rise up
so powerfully that they stop, glowing
      in their heart's abundance,
while, like the soft night air, the temp-
      tation to blossom
touches their tender mouths, touches
      their eyelids, softly:
heroes perhaps, and those chosen to
      disappear early,
whose veins Death the gardener twists
      into a different pattern.
These plunge on ahead: in advance of
      their own smile
like the team of galloping horses be-
      fore the triumphant
pharaoh in the mildly hollowed reliefs
      at Karnak.

The hero is strangely close to those
    who died young. Permanence
does not concern him. He lives in
    continual ascent,
moving on into the ever-changed
    constellation
of perpetual danger. Few could find
    him there. But
Fate, which is silent about us, suddenly
    grows inspired
and sings him into the storm of his
    onrushing world.
I hear no one like *him*. All at once I
    am pierced
by his darkened voice, carried on the
    streaming air.

Then how gladly I would hide from
    the longing to be once again
oh a boy once again, with my life be-
    fore me, to sit

leaning on future arms and reading
    of Samson,
how from his mother first nothing,
    then everything, was born.

Wasn't he a hero inside you, mother?
    didn't
his imperious choosing already begin
    there, in you?
Thousands seethed in your womb,
    wanting to be *him,*
but look: he grasped and excluded—,
    chose and prevailed.
And if he demolished pillars, it was
    when he burst
from the world of your body into the
    narrower world, where again
he chose and prevailed. O mothers of
    heroes, O sources
of ravaging floods! You ravines into
    which
virgins have plunged, lamenting,

from the highest rim of the heart,
    sacrifices to the son.
  For whenever the hero stormed
    through the stations of love,
each heartbeat intended for him lifted
    him up, beyond it;
and, turning away, he stood there,
    at the end of all smiles,
      —transfigured.

THE SEVENTH ELEGY

Not wooing, no longer shall wooing,
    voice that has outgrown it,
be the nature of your cry; but instead,
    you would cry out as purely as
    a bird
when the quickly ascending season lifts
    him up, nearly forgetting
that he is a suffering creature and not
    just a single heart
being flung into brightness, into the
    intimate skies. Just like him
you would be wooing, not any less
    purely—, so that, still
unseen, she would sense you, the silent
    lover in whom a reply
slowly awakens and, as she hears you,
    grows warm,—

and shine with beginning.
Not only the days, so tender around
flowers and, above,
around the patterned treetops, so
strong, so intense.
Not only the reverence of all these
unfolded powers,
not only the pathways, not only the
meadows at sunset,
not only, after a late storm, the
deep-breathing freshness,
not only approaching sleep, and a
premonition . . .
but also the nights! But also the lofty
summer
nights, and the stars as well, the stars
of the earth.
Oh to be dead at last and know them
endlessly,
all the stars: for how, how could we
ever forget them!

the ardent companion to your own
    most daring emotion.

Oh and springtime would hold it—,
    everywhere it would echo
the song of annunciation. First the
    small
questioning notes intensified all around
by the sheltering silence of a pure,
    affirmative day.
Then up the stairs, up the stairway of
    calls, to the dreamed-of
temple of the future—, and then the
    trill, like a fountain
which, in its rising jet, already anti-
    cipates its fall
in a game of promises . . . . And still
    ahead: summer.
  Not only all the dawns of summer—,
    not only
how they change themselves into day

Look, I was calling for my lover. But
    not just *she*
would come . . . Out of their fragile
    graves
girls would arise and gather . . . For
    how could I limit
the call, once I called it? These unripe
    spirits keep seeking
the earth.—Children, one earthly
    Thing
truly experienced, even once, is
    enough for a lifetime.
Don't think that fate is more than
    the density of childhood;
how often you outdistanced the man
    you loved, breathing, breathing
after the blissful chase, and passed on
    into freedom.

Truly being here is glorious. Even *you*
    knew it,

you girls who seemed to be lost, to go
    under—, in the filthiest
streets of the city, festering there, or
    wide open
for garbage. For each of you had an
    hour, or perhaps
not even an hour, a barely measurable
    time
between two moments—, when you
    were granted a sense
of being. Everything. Your veins flowed
    with being.
But we can so easily forget what our
    laughing neighbor
neither confirms nor envies. We want
    to display it,
to make it visible, though even the
    most visible happiness
can't reveal itself to us until we trans-
    form it, within.
Nowhere, Beloved, will world be but
    within us. Our life

passes in transformation. And the ex-
     ternal
shrinks into less and less. Where once
     an enduring house was,
now a cerebral structure crosses our
     path, completely
belonging to the realm of concepts, as
     though it still stood in the brain.
Our age has built itself vast reservoirs
     of power,
formless as the straining energy that it
     wrests from the earth.
Temples are no longer known. It is we
     who secretly save up
these extravagances of the heart.
     Where one of them still survives,
a Thing that was formerly prayed to,
     worshipped, knelt before —
just as it is, it passes into the invisible
     world.
Many no longer perceive it, yet miss
     the chance

to build it *inside* themselves now, with
    pillars and statues: greater.

Each torpid turn of the world has such
    disinherited ones,
to whom neither the past belongs, nor
    yet what has nearly arrived.
For even the nearest moment is far
    from mankind. Though *we*
should not be confused by this, but
    strengthened in our task of pre-
      serving
the still-recognizable form. — This
    once *stood* among mankind,
in the midst of Fate the annihilator, in
    the midst
of Not-Knowing-Whither, it stood as
    if enduring, and bent
stars down to it from their safeguarded
    heavens. Angel,
to *you* I will show it, *there!* in your end-
    less vision

it shall stand, now finally upright,
    rescued at last.
Pillars, pylons, the Sphinx, the striving
    thrust
of the cathedral, gray, from a fading or
    alien city.

Wasn't all this a miracle? Be aston-
    ished, Angel, for we
are this, O Great One; proclaim that
    we could achieve this, my breath
is too short for such praise. So, after
    all, we have not
failed to make use of these generous
    spaces, these
spaces of *ours.* (How frighteningly
    great they must be,
since thousands of years have not made
    them overflow with our feelings.)
But a tower was great, wasn't it? Oh
    Angel, it was—
even when placed beside you? Chartres

was great—, and music
reached still higher and passed far be-
    yond us. But even
a woman in love—, oh alone at night
    by her window. . . .
didn't she reach your knee—?
        Don't think that I'm wooing.
Angel, and even if I were, you would
    not come. For my call
is always filled with departure; against
    such a powerful
current you cannot move. Like an out-
    stretched arm
is my call. And its hand, held open and
    reaching up
to seize, remains in front of you, open
as if in defense and warning,
Ungraspable One, far above.

THE EIGHTH ELEGY

Dedicated to Rudolf Kassner

With all its eyes the natural world
    looks out
into the Open. Only *our* eyes are
    turned
backward, and surround plant, animal,
    child
like traps, as they emerge into their
    freedom.
We know what is really out there
    only from
the animal's gaze; for we take the
    very young
child and force it around, so that it
    sees
objects—not the Open, which is so

deep in animals' faces. Free from
    death.
We, only, can see death; the free
    animal
has its decline in back of it, forever,
and God in front, and when it moves,
    it moves
already in eternity, like a fountain.
    Never, not for a single day, do *we*
    have
before us that pure space into which
    flowers
endlessly open. Always there is World
and never Nowhere without the No:
    that pure
unseparated element which one
    breathes
without desire and endlessly *knows*.
    A child
may wander there for hours, through
    the timeless
stillness, may get lost in it and be

shaken back. Or someone dies and
    is it.
For, nearing death, one doesn't see
    death; but stares
beyond, perhaps with an animal's
    vast gaze.
Lovers, if the beloved were not there
blocking the view, are close to it, and
    marvel . . .
As if by some mistake, it opens for
    them
behind each other . . . But neither
    can move past
the other, and it changes back to
    World.
Forever turned toward objects, we see
    in them
the mere reflection of the realm of
    freedom,
which we have dimmed. Or when
    some animal

mutely, serenely, looks us through
    and through.
That is what fate means: to be op-
    posite,
to be opposite and nothing else,
    forever.

If the animal moving toward us so
    securely
in a different direction had our kind
    of
consciousness—, it would wrench us
    around and drag us
along its path. But it feels its life as
    boundless,
unfathomable, and without regard
to its own condition: pure, like its
    outward gaze.
And where we see the future, it sees
    all time
and itself within all time, forever
    healed.

Yet in the alert, warm animal there lies
the pain and burden of an enormous
    sadness.
For it too feels the presence of what
    often
overwhelms us: a memory, as if
the element we keep pressing toward
    was once
more intimate, more true, and our
    communion
infinitely tender. Here all is distance;
there it was breath. After that first
    home,
the second seems ambiguous and
    drafty.
  Oh bliss of the *tiny* creature which
    remains
forever inside the womb that was its
    shelter;
joy of the gnat which, still *within,*
    leaps up

even at its marriage: for everything
is womb.
And look at the half-assurance of
the bird,
which knows both inner and outer,
from its source,
as if it were the soul of an Etruscan,
flown out of a dead man received
inside a space,
but with his reclining image as the lid.
And how bewildered is any womb-
born creature
that has to fly. As if terrified and
fleeing
from itself, it zigzags through the air,
the way
a crack runs through a teacup. So
the bat
quivers across the porcelain of evening.

And we: spectators, always, every-
where,

turned toward the world of objects,
    never outward.
It fills us. We arrange it. It breaks
    down.
We rearrange it, then break down
    ourselves.

Who has twisted us around like this,
    so that
no matter what we do, we are in the
    posture
of someone going away? Just as, upon
the farthest hill, which shows him his
    whole valley
one last time, he turns, stops, lin-
    gers—,
so we live here, forever taking leave.

THE NINTH ELEGY

Why, if this interval of being can be
    spent serenely
in the form of a laurel, slightly darker
    than all
other green, with tiny waves on the
    edges
of every leaf (like the smile of a
    breeze)—: why then
have to be human—and, escaping
    from fate,
keep longing for fate? . . .

    Oh *not* because happiness *exists*,
that too-hasty profit snatched from
    approaching loss.
Not out of curiosity, not as practice
    for the heart, which

would exist in the laurel too . . . . .

But because *truly* being here is so
    much; because everything here
apparently needs us, this fleeting
    world, which in some strange
    way
keeps calling to us. Us, the most
    fleeting of all.
Once for each thing. Just once; no
    more. And we too,
just once. And never again. But to
    have been
this once, completely, even if only
    once:
to have been at one with the earth,
    seems beyond undoing.

And so we keep pressing on, trying to
    achieve it,
trying to hold it firmly in our simple
    hands,

in our overcrowded gaze, in our
    speechless heart.
Trying to become it.—Whom can we
    give it to? We would
hold on to it all, forever . . . Ah, but
    what can we take along
into that other realm? Not the art of
    looking,
which is learned so slowly, and
    nothing that happened here.
    Nothing.
The sufferings, then. And, above all,
    the heaviness,
and the long experience of love,—
    just what is wholly
unsayable. But later, among the stars,
what good is it—*they* are *better* as
    they are: unsayable.
For when the traveler returns from the
    mountain-slopes into the valley,
he brings, not a handful of earth,
    unsayable to others, but instead

some word he has gained, some pure
    word, the yellow and blue
gentian. Perhaps we are *here* in order
    to say: house,
bridge, fountain, gate, pitcher, fruit-
    tree, window—
at most: column, tower. . . . But to *say*
    them, you must understand,
oh to say them *more* intensely than the
    Things themselves
ever dreamed of existing. Isn't the
    secret intent
of this taciturn earth, when it forces
    lovers together,
that inside their boundless emotion all
    things may shudder with joy?
Threshold: what it means for two
    lovers
to be wearing down, imperceptibly,
    the ancient threshold of their
    door—

they too, after the many who came
    before them
and before those to come . . . . ,
    lightly.

Here is the time for the *sayable, here* is
    its homeland.
Speak and bear witness. More than
    ever
the Things that we might experience
    are vanishing, for
what crowds them out and replaces
    them is an imageless act.
An act under a shell, which easily
    cracks open as soon as
the business inside outgrows it and
    seeks new limits.
Between the hammers our heart
endures, just as the tongue does
between the teeth and, despite that,
still is able to praise.

Praise this world to the angel, not the
    unsayable one,
you can't impress *him* with glorious
    emotion; in the universe
where he feels more powerfully, you
    are a novice. So show him
something simple which, formed over
    generations,
lives as our own, near our hand and
    within our gaze.
Tell him of Things. He will stand as-
    tonished; as *you* stood
by the rope-maker in Rome or the
    potter along the Nile.
Show him how happy a Thing can be,
    how innocent and ours,
how even lamenting grief purely de-
    cides to take form,
serves as a Thing, or dies into a
    Thing—, and blissfully
escapes far beyond the violin.—And
    these Things,

which live by perishing, know you are
praising them; transient,
they look to us for deliverance: us, the
most transient of all.´
They want us to change them, utterly,
in our invisible heart,
within—oh endlessly—within us!
Whoever we may be at last.

Earth, isn't this what you want: to
arise within us,
invisible? Isn't it your dream
to be wholly invisible someday?
—O Earth: invisible!
What, if not transformation, is your
urgent command?
Earth, my dearest, I will. Oh believe
me, you no longer
need your springtimes to win me
over—one of them,
ah, even one, is already too much for
my blood.

Unspeakably I have belonged to you,
    from the first.
You were always right, and your holiest
    inspiration
is our intimate companion, Death.

Look, I am living. On what? Neither
    childhood nor future
grows any smaller . . . . . Superabundant
    being
wells up in my heart.

THE TENTH ELEGY

Someday, emerging at last from the
       violent insight,
let me sing out jubilation and praise
       to assenting angels.
Let not even one of the clearly struck
       hammers of my heart
fail to sound because of a slack, a
       doubtful,
or a broken string. Let my joyfully
       streaming face
make me more radiant; let my hidden
       weeping arise
and blossom. How dear you will be
       to me then, you nights
of anguish. Why didn't I kneel more
       deeply to accept you,

inconsolable sisters, and, surrendering,
    lose myself
in your loosened hair. How we
    squander our hours of pain.
How we gaze beyond them into the
    bitter duration
to see if they have an end. Though
    they are really
our winter-enduring foliage, our dark
    evergreen,
one season in our inner year—, not
    only a season
in time—, but are place and settle-
    ment, foundation and soil and
    home.

But how alien, alas, are the streets
    of the city of grief,
where, in the false silence formed of
    continual uproar,
the figure cast from the mold of emp-
    tiness stoutly

swaggers: the gilded noise, the burst-
      ing memorial.
Oh how completely an angel would
      stamp out their market of solace,
bounded by the church with its ready-
      made consolations:
clean and disenchanted and shut as a
      post-office on Sunday.
Farther out, though, the city's edges
      are curling with carnival.
Swings of freedom! Divers and jugglers
      of zeal!
And the shooting-gallery's targets of
      prettified happiness,
which jump and kick back with a
      tinny sound
when hit by some better marksman.
      From cheers to chance
he goes staggering on, as booths with
      all sorts of attractions
are wooing, drumming, and bawling.
      For adults only

there is something special to see: how
money multiplies, naked,
right there on stage, money's genitals,
nothing concealed,
the whole action—, educational, and
guaranteed
to increase your potency . . . .
. . . . Oh, but a little farther,
beyond the last of the billboards, plas-
tered with signs for
"Deathless,"
that bitter beer which seems so sweet
to its drinkers
as long as they chew fresh distractions
in between sips . . . ,
just in back of the billboard, just behind, the view becomes *real*.
Children are playing, and lovers are
holding hands, to the side,
solemnly in the meager grass, and dogs
are doing what is natural.
The young man is drawn on, farther;

perhaps he is in love with a
        young
Lament . . . . . He comes out behind
        her, into the meadows. She says:
—It's a long walk. We live way out
        there . . . .
                Where? And the youth
follows. He is touched by her manner,
        Her shoulders, her neck—,
        perhaps
she is of noble descent. But he leaves
        her, turns around,
looks back, waves . . . What's the use?
        She is a Lament.

Only those who died young, in their
        first condition
of timeless equanimity, while they are
        being weaned,
follow her lovingly. She waits
for girls and befriends them. Shows
        them, gently,

what she is wearing. Pearls of grief and
    the fine-spun
veils of patience.— With young men
    she walks
in silence.

But there, in the valley, where they
    live, one of the elder Laments
answers the youth when he questions
    her:—Long ago,
she says, we Laments were a powerful
    race. Our forefathers worked
the mines, up there in the mountain-
    range; sometimes even
among men you can find a polished
    nugget of primal grief
or a chunk of petrified rage from the
    slag of an ancient volcano.
Yes, that came from up there. We used
    to be rich.—

And gently she guides him through
    the vast landscape of Lament,
shows him the pillars of the temples,
    and the ruined walls
of those castles from which, long ago,
    the princes of Lament
wisely ruled the land. Shows him the
    tall
trees of tears and the fields of blos-
    soming grief
(the living know it just as a mild green
    shrub);
shows him the herds of sorrow, graz-
    ing,   and sometimes
a startled bird, flying low through their
    upward gaze,
far away traces the image of its solitary
    cry. —
In the twilight she leads him out to the
    graves of the elders
who gave warning to the race of La-
    ments, the sibyls and prophets.

But as night approaches, they move
        more softly, and soon
the sepulchre rises up
like a moon, watching over everything.
        Brother to the one on the Nile,
the lofty Sphinx —: the taciturn
        chamber's
countenance.
And they look in wonder at the regal
        head that has silently
lifted the human face
to the scale of the stars, forever.

Still dizzy from recent death, his sight
cannot grasp it. But her gaze
frightens an owl from behind the rim
        of the crown. And the bird,
with slow downstrokes, brushes along
        the cheek,
the one with the fuller curve,
and faintly, in the dead youth's new
sense of hearing, as upon a double

unfolded page, it sketches the inde-
scribable outline.
And higher, the stars. The new stars
of the land of grief.
Slowly the Lament names them:—
Look, there:
the *Rider,* the *Staff,* and the larger constellation
called *Garland of Fruit.* Then, farther up
toward the Pole:
*Cradle; Path; The Burning Book; Puppet;
Window.*
But there, in the southern sky, pure as
the lines
on the palm of a blessed hand, the
clear sparkling *M*
that stands for Mothers . . . . . . —

But the dead youth must go on by
himself, and silently the elder
Lament

takes him as far as the ravine,
where shimmering in the moonlight
is the fountainhead of joy. With rev-
    erence
she names it and says: — Among men
it is a mighty stream. —

They stand at the foot of the moun-
    tain-range.
And she embraces him, weeping.

Alone, he climbs on, up the mountains
    of primal grief.
And not once do his footsteps echo
    from the soundless path.

*

But if the endlessly dead awakened a
        symbol in us,
perhaps they would point to the catkins
        hanging from the bare
    branches of the hazel-trees, or

would evoke the raindrops that fall onto
    the dark earth in springtime. —

And we, who have always thought
of happiness as *rising*, would feel
the emotion that almost overwhelms us
whenever a happy thing *falls*.

APPENDIX

[FRAGMENT OF AN ELEGY]

Now shall I praise the cities, those
    long-surviving
(I watched them in awe) great con-
    stellations of earth.
For only in praising is my heart still
    mine, so violently
do I know the world. And even my
    lament
turns into a paean before my dis-
    consolate heart.
Let no one say that I don't love life,
    the eternal
presence: I pulsate in her; she bears
    me, she gives me
the spaciousness of this day, the
    primeval workday

for me to make use of, and over my
    existence flings,
in her magnanimity, nights that have
    never been.
Her strong hand is above me, and if
    she should hold me under,
submerged in fate, I would have to
    learn how to breathe
down there. Even her most lightly-
    entrusted mission
would fill me with songs of her; al-
    though I suspect
that all she wants is for me to be
    vibrant as she is.
Once poets resounded over the battle-
    field; what voice
can outshout the rattle of this metallic
    age
that is struggling on toward its ca-
    reening future?
And indeed it hardly requires the call,
    its own battle-din

roars into song. So let me stand for
    a while
in front of the transient: not accusing,
    but once again
admiring, marveling. And if perhaps
    something founders
before my eyes and stirs me into la-
    ment,
it is not a reproach. Why shouldn't
    more youthful nations
rush past the graveyard of cultures
    long ago rotten?
How pitiful it would be if greatness
    needed the slightest
indulgence. Let him whose soul is no
    longer startled
and transformed by palaces, by gar-
    dens' boldness, by the rising
and falling of ancient fountains, by
    everything held back
in paintings or by the infinite thereness
    of statues—

let such a person go out to his daily
    work, where
greatness is lying in ambush and
    someday, at some turn,
will leap upon him and force him to
    fight for his life.

[ORIGINAL VERSION OF THE TENTH ELEGY]

[Fragmentary]

Someday, emerging at last from the
    violent insight,
let me sing out jubilation and praise to
    assenting angels.
Let not even one of the clearly-struck
    hammers of my heart
fail to sound because of a slack, a
    doubtful,
or an ill-tempered string. Let my joy-
    fully streaming face
make me more radiant; let my hidden
    weeping arise
and blossom. How dear you will be to
    me then, you nights

of anguish. Why didn't I kneel more
    deeply to accept you,
inconsolable sisters, and, surrendering,
    lose myself
in your loosened hair. How we squan-
    der our hours of pain.
How we gaze beyond them into the
    bitter duration
to see if they have an end. Though
    they are really
seasons of us, our winter-
enduring foliage, ponds, meadows, our
    inborn landscape,
where birds and reed-dwelling crea-
    tures are at home.

High overhead, isn't half of the night
    sky standing
above the sorrow in us, the disquieted
    garden?
Imagine that you no longer walked
    through your grief grown wild,

no longer looked at the stars through
    the jagged leaves
of the dark tree of pain, and the en-
    larging moonlight
no longer exalted fate's ruins so high
that among them you felt like the last
    of some ancient race.
Nor would smiles any longer exist,
    the consuming smiles
of those you lost over there—with so
    little violence,
once they were past, did they purely
    enter your grief.
(Almost like the girl who has just said
    yes to the lover
who begged her, so many weeks, and
    she brings him astonished
to the garden gate and, reluctant, he
    walks away,
giddy with joy; and then, amid this
    new parting,

a step disturbs her; she waits; and her
    glance in its fullness
sinks totally into a stranger's: her vir-
    gin glance
that endlessly comprehends him, the
    outsider, who was meant for her;
the wandering other, who eternally
    was meant for her.
Echoing, he walks by.) That is how,
    always, you lost:
never as one who possesses, but like
    someone dying
who, bending into the moist breeze
    of an evening in March,
loses the springtime, alas, in the
    throats of the birds.

Far too much you belong to grief. If
    you could forget her—
even the least of these figures so in-
    finitely pained—
you would call down, shout down,

        hoping they might still be
        curious,
one of the angels (those beings un-
        mighty in grief)
who, as his face darkened, would try
        again and again
to describe the way you kept sobbing,
        long ago, for her.
Angel, what was it like? And he would
        imitate you and never
understand that it was pain, as after a
        calling bird
one tries to repeat the innocent voice
        it is filled with.

ANTISTROPHES

Ah, Women, that you should be
        moving
here, among us, grief-filled,
no more protected than we, and
        nevertheless
able to bless like the blessed.

From what realm,
when your beloved appears,
do you take the future?
More than will ever be.
One who knows distances
out to the outermost star
is astonished when he discovers
the magnificent space in your hearts.
How, in the crowd, can you spare it?
You, full of sources and night.

Are you really the same
as those children who
on the way to school were rudely
shoved by an older brother?
Unharmed by it.

> While we, even as children,
> disfigured ourselves forever,
> you were like bread on the altar
> before it is changed.

The breaking away of childhood
left you intact. In a moment,
you stood there, as if completed
in a miracle, all at once.

> We, as if broken from crags,
> even as boys, too sharp
> at the edges, although perhaps
> sometimes skillfully cut;
> we, like pieces of rock
> that have fallen on flowers.

Flowers of the deeper soil,
loved by all roots,
you, Eurydice's sisters,
full of holy return
behind the ascending man.

   We, afflicted by ourselves,
   gladly afflicting, gladly
   needing to be afflicted.
   We, who sleep with our anger
   laid beside us like a knife.

You, who are almost protection
where no one protects. The thought
     of you
is a shade-giving tree of sleep for the
     restless
creatures of a solitary man.

ABOUT THE COVER

The painting *La Famille des Saltimbanques* by Pablo Picasso served as one of Rilke's principle sources of inspiration for the Fifth Elegy. The painting made such a deep impression on Rilke that he wrote to the owner, Frau Hertha Koenig, asking if he could stay in her Munich home while she was away for the summer of 1915, so that he could live beneath the great work, "which gives me the courage for this request." The request was granted, and Rilke spent four months in the presence of the "glorious Picasso."

With the completion of the Fifth Elegy (the last one chronologically), Rilke wrote, "Only now does the circle of the Elegies seem to me truly closed."

LIBRARY OF CONGRESS
CATALOGING-IN-PUBLICATION DATA

Rilke, Rainer Maria, 1875–1926.
[Duineser Elegien. English]
Duino elegies/Rainer Maria Rilke;
translated by Stephen Mitchell.
— 1st Shambhala ed.
p.   cm. — (Shambhala pocket classics)
Translation of: Duineser Elegien.
ISBN 0 87773-852-1 (alk. paper)
I. Mitchell, Stephen, 1943–
II. Title.   III. Series.
PT2635.I65D82   1992   92-50121
831'.912—dc20   CIP